YA TE VEO

Miller Williams Poetry Series
EDITED BY BILLY COLLINS

Ya Te Veo

POEMS BY
P. Scott Cunningham

The University of Arkansas Press
Fayetteville
2018

ISBN: 978-1-68226-056-2
eISBN: 978-1-61075-632-7

22 21 20 19 18   5 4 3 2 1

Designed by Liz Lester

⊗ The paper used in this publication meets the mini-
mum requirements of the American National Standard
for Permanence of Paper for Printed Library Materials
Z39.48–1984

Library of Congress Control Number: 2017956140

Series Editor's Preface

When the University of Arkansas Press asked if I would act as editor for the coming year's annual poetry prize named in honor of Miller Williams—the long-time director of the press and its poetry program—I was quick to accept. Since 1988 when he published my first full-length book, *The Apple That Astonished Paris*, I have felt indebted to Miller, who died in January 2015 at the age of eighty-four. From the beginning of his time at the press, it was Miller's practice to publish one poet's first book every year. Then in 1990 this commitment was formalized when Miller awarded the first Arkansas Poetry Prize. Fittingly, it was renamed the Miller Williams Poetry Prize after his retirement.

When Miller first spotted my poetry, I was forty-six years old with two chapbooks only. Not a pretty sight.

I have him to thank for first carrying me across that critical line dividing *no book* from *book*, thus turning me, at last, into a "published poet." I was especially eager to take on the task of selecting books (with the assistance of many invaluable screeners) for the Miller Williams Poetry Prize because it is a publication prize, which may bring to light other first books.

Miller Williams was more than my first editor. Over the years, he and I became friends, but even before my involvement with the press, he served as a kind of literary father to me. His straightforward, sometimes folksy, sometimes witty and always trenchant poems became to me models of how poems could sound and how they could go. He was one of the poets who showed me that humor could be a legitimate mode in poetry—that a poem could be humorous without being silly or merely comical. He also showed me that a plain-spoken poem did not have to be imaginatively plain. Younger poets today could learn much from his example, as I did.

Given his extensive and distinguished career, it's surprising that Miller didn't enjoy a more prominent position on the

American literary map. As his daughter became well-known as a singer and recording artist, Miller became known to many as the father of Lucinda Williams. Miller and Lucinda even appeared on stage together several times performing a father-daughter act of song and poetry. And Miller enjoyed a bright, shining moment when Bill Clinton chose him to be the inaugural poet at his second inauguration in 1997. The poem he wrote for that day, "Of History and Hope," is a meditation on how "we have memorized America." In turning to the children of our country he broadens a nursery rhyme question by asking "How does our garden grow?" Occasional poems, especially for occasions of such importance, are notoriously difficult—some would say impossible—to write with success. But Miller rose to this lofty occasion and produced a winner. His confident reading of the poem before the nation added cultural and emotional weight to the morning's ceremony.

Apart from such public recognitions, most would agree that Miller's fuller legacy lies in his teaching and publishing career, which covered four decades. In that time, he published over a dozen books of his own poetry and literary theory. His literary work as poet and editor is what will speak for Miller in the years to come. The qualities of his poems make them immediately likeable and pleasurable. They sound as if they were spoken, not just written, and they show a courteous, engaging awareness of the presence of a reader. Miller knew that the idea behind a good poem is to make the reader feel something, rather than to merely display the poet's emotional state, which usually boils down to some form of misery. Miller also possessed the authority of experience to produce poems that were just plain wise.

With these attributes in mind, I began the judging of this year's prize. On the lookout for poems that Miller would approve of, that is, poems that seemed to be consciously or unconsciously in the Miller Williams School, I read and read. But in reading these scores of manuscripts, I realized that applying such narrow criteria would be selling Miller short. His tastes in poetry were clearly broader than the stylistic territory of his own verse; he published poets as different from one another as John Ciardi and Jimmy Carter. I read-justed and began to look for poems I thought Miller would delight in reading, instead of echoes of his own poems. Broadening the field of judgment brought happy results. It took some second-guessing, but I'm confident that Miller would enthusiastically approve of this year's selections. The work of three very different poets, who have readability, freshness of language, and seriousness of intent in common, stood out from the stack of submissions.

Roy Bentley is a child of the movies. In one of the poems in *Walking with Eve in the Loved City*, this self-described "fat-kid eighth grader" is watching *Bullitt* for the third time straight while an impartial usher looks on. The distance between this Ohio boy stuffing himself with popcorn and Steve McQueen gunning his Mustang GT 390 collapses as the poem rises to an ecstatic celebration of "a communion of terrific car chases wherein thunderous / algorithms of horsepower rule." In another poem, the hormonal uptick of adolescence caused by attending "Sex Ed classes / with our dads" is registered while the speaker watches *Son of Frankenstein* in his "pj's at Gary Laberman's house on Comanche Drive." When he and his friends become sexually active, the poet is certain, "townspeople will start lighting torches." These poems get where they're going by way of long, loopy sentences dotted with references to high and low culture. Helpfully, Bentley is fond of titles that inform and orient the reader rather than obstruct entry to the poem. I appreciated "Saturday Afternoon at the Midland Theatre in Newark, Ohio" almost as much as I did "Ringo Starr Answers Questions on *Larry King Live* about the Death of George Harrison." And poems about Rimbaud and Robert E. Lee anchor us in history then set us adrift in the poet's revisionist take on these glorified figures. This is a lively collection that instructs, delights, and uplifts.

When asked how to account for the distinctive guitar work of the Rolling Stones, Ron Wood said, "I think it's a bit like the ancient art of weaving." This is a skill that Scott Cunningham knows well (and even acknowledges in an epigraph), for several of his poems make a variety of designs by braiding together strands of their own lines. In one poem titled "Fugue 52" (implying there are more to come), and in another, a sonnet sequence titled "Now a Word about Twentieth-Century Music," repeated lines are used as threads and connective tissue to hold the poems in tight order. That Morton Feldman, the composer, makes Zelig-like appearances in both of these poems should come as no coincidence because the poems themselves exhibit a musical structure, though thankfully not as complexly experimental as that of a Feldman composition. The collection, *Ya Te Veo,* offers many other delights including a wiggy explanation of how the New York School was formed and an updated, parodic version of "Dover Beach" that comes out of the box with "The sea is a bomb tonight." Also notable is a poem about a victim of the Salem witch trials, Giles Corey, who was put to death by a now mercifully shelved method called "pressing," in which the victim lies under a board, which is then loaded with heavier and heavier stones until a confession or death is achieved. "More weight," Corey memorably demands from his execution-ers. And don't miss "Poems about Concentration for People Who Can't Concentrate," perhaps a distant cousin of Geoff Dyer's essay collection *Yoga for People Who Can't be Bothered to Do It.* A sample: "You're at your desk. / You can't concentrate. / Imagine if not concentrating / was concentrating." In sum, a distinctive collection by a very savvy poet.

What often lures us into poems and keeps our interest is the poet's sensibility, that intangible element that arises from a poet's tone, his or her verbal personality. That is what hooked me when I began to read *Narcissus Americana.* Travis Mossotti's tone is a mixture of irony and true feeling, or rather a balancing act between the cool of one and the warmth of the other. Here's a poet who laments the absence of poets getting drunk in their poems, "like William Matthews did." A smart, informed melancholia can be found in many of these poems, including an exclamatory ode to condoms that is peppered with Shelley-like Os, and a poem detail-ing an encounter at a concert with a woman whose life and body are ruined by meth—a poem that ends surprisingly with the ceiling of the famous chapel whose name rhymes with hers: *Christine*. I trust this poet who can tell the tenor from the vehicle and whose poem "Cigar" shows us that many times a cigar is not just a cigar. Mossotti can also produce a narrative adventure, as he does in "Abandoned Quarry," where diving underwater at night conveys a cinematic level of excitement and tension. Producing poems that are clear and mysterious, funny and serious, Travis Mossotti is one of a thriving group of American poets writing these days whose work exposes the mendacity of those who cite "difficulty" as an excuse for not reading poetry.

In short, we have here a gathering of poets whose work, I think, would have fully engaged and gladdened Miller Williams. Because I have sat with him there, I can picture Miller in his study turning these pages, maybe stopping to make a pencil note in a margin. Miller's hope, of course, was that the poems published in this series would find a broad readership, ready to be delighted and inspired. I join my old friend and editor in that wish.

Billy Collins

Acknowledgments

My deepest gratitude to the journals in which some of these poems originally appeared, sometimes with different titles and forms: *Abe's Penny*, "Dear Goose"; *A Public Space*, "Giles Corey"; *Cartridge Lit*, "There Is a Forward Motion in Old Video Games"; *Columbia: A Journal of Literature and Art*, "Soda Can"; *Floating Wolf Quarterly*, "Now a Word about Twentieth-Century Music"; *Harvard Review*, "Leica"; *International Literary Quarterly*, "January in Buffalo"; *La Otra*, "I Drank Some Milk and It Rained"; *Maggy*, "Against Detroit," "Against Surrealism," "How the New York School Was Formed"; *Okey-Panky*, "Bidart & Lowell," "Noir," "Florida Man," "Dover Beaches," "Wagner & Nietzsche"; *PANK*, "Poems about Concentration for People Who Can't Concentrate"; *Pool: A Journal of Poetry*, "Fugue 52"; *The Pure Francis*, "O, 1951"; *Redivider*, "Examining a Carpet"; *RHINO*, "Planet Earth"; *Rumpus*, "Jack Gilbert"; *Sou'wester*, "O, 1987"; *Swamp Ape Review*, "Three Plants That Eat People"; *Tupelo Quarterly*, "A Story about a Marriage."

Thank you to Billy Collins and to the editors and staff at the University of Arkansas Press; Campbell McGrath, Denise Duhamel, and the entire creative writing family at Florida International University. Thank you to everyone who lent a hand to this manuscript, but especially: Sarah Trudgeon, Cherry Pickman, Frank Bidart, Adrian Matejka, Major Jackson, Gabrielle Calvocoressi, Chloe Garcia Roberts, Kevin Young, and Roger Reeves. Dalé to the O, Miami and Jai-Alai Books family. Thank you to all my friends but especially to Seth Labenz for the real genius of his design and to Nathaniel Sandler for giving me all of his best ideas for free. Most of all, thank you to my family for their love and support: Rod, Carolyn, Sarah, and the rest of the Cunninghams; the Wesselhoff and Frigo clans; my love, Ada, and my greatest love, Christina.

Contents

Don't let it end like this. Tell them I said something.

—THE LAST WORDS OF PANCHO VILLA

YA TE VEO

Giles Corey

In Massachusetts, they made a pile of stones
to lay, one by one, onto his chest.
With each stone they placed, they asked,
like game show hosts, *Do you confess?*

When he refused to respond, they got angry,
like plainclothes cops taking off their jackets.
Do you understand the stakes, Giles?
Do you realize the wealth of stones

God has given to this township?
We can do this all day, they said,
and by not answering, Giles held them to it.
Killing him was like being at a dinner party

at which the host refuses to go to bed.
People excused themselves to go to the bathroom.
They got hungry and ordered out. They dozed off and woke up
inside the soft glow of the television.

After a day and a half, no one could remember
the right order in which things happened. No one
had thought to keep track of what went first, or who did what.
The world started to resemble a pile of stuff

they'd floated into by accident.
Whose absence is this? they wondered.
Are we its creator or its instrument?
In the beginning there was nothing, and God said,

That's not enough, and then there was
the stone-pile Giles looked up from under.
There was the sky above him, and soon
it began to change colors—brown to red to black.

It was a thing he could control by blinking his eyes.
Every breath arrived like a letter.
His head had become a kind of stone.
More weight, he said.

Planet Earth

*. . . The variety of ephemera of human intervention
on the landscape is far greater than anything the
land itself has to offer.*

—WILLIAM KENTRIDGE

I.

Summer. Men emerge from garages
dragging cans of gasoline and chainsaws
into the trees. Like most things, trees can
sometimes look like people. They scream
Get off of me! Except they don't.
They take their trimming like a human.
Like birds, chainsaws have eyes—
one on each side of the head, lidded
by the heavy chain that winks as it spins,
throwing its nose over and over into the heart
of the trunk. Each saw, once ignited,
works furiously to exhaust itself, emitting
in the open air a horrible noise
no one can stand, least of all the saw—
Has anyone seen my glasses? it says.
But what it sounds like once it's in the tree
is the opposite: saw and tree become
the same, so if sound contains truth,
then trees were made to be cut down.
Have you ever heard one fall? The wood
cracks and breaks with *full-throated ease.*

II.

Airplanes fly. As businesses, they fail.
People get into them, are vaulted five
miles into the sky, then fall asleep.
In 1978, 1% of couples met on planes.
Despite what you've been told, falling in love
requires speaking. He saw her first
in the boarding area, kneeling, then
she was across the aisle. Speaking
felt like pounding in a flush nail.
They wrote letters for a year. He drove
down the mountain to the post office
every day, and when the box was empty
he assumed he'd said too much.
When it wasn't, he opened the envelope
walking through the parking lot.
In person, they lasted one month before
he cheated on her with a woman who sold
running shoes you weren't supposed to run in.
There's a difference between elegance
and truth. Airplanes land on wheels.

III.

Once, in the woods, I saw two owls mate.
At first I saw only one, standing in a tree.
The noise it made was deep and powerful.
Snow and leaf were a cathedral I crawled
through to be closer to the sound. The light
was fading and I was just about to go
when a reply came from the canopy.
Like waves breaking into one another, each cry
punished the air, each had its own mass
that rolled across the world and crashed
into the bird it had been aimed at.
Each cry arrived faster than the one before
until every other sound had been flattened
and the other, with the violence of a planet,
burst into the clearing. With each flap
it halved the distance between them until
one was hovering over the other.
Each bird was airborne now, suspended by
the weight of its alternate. Neither made
a sound. I held my breath until it burned.

Three Plants That Eat People

I. *Ya Te Veo*

> *The ya-te-veo ("now-I-see-you") plant is said to*
> *catch and consume large insects but also attempts*
> *to consume humans.*
> —J. W. BUEL, *SEA & LAND* (1887)

Beside the road, a tree. Someone passes,
gets eaten. Another passes and is
eaten too. Another stops to take a nap
beneath the leaves, and gets robbed
and beaten by crooks. Before
he leaves, he picks a piece of fruit.

By choosing who to eat, the tree
stays hidden. There it is in many paintings—
wind fed, sunlight breaking inside of it—
in the distance, a ship or two, some birds.
At first the tree was gnarled and covered
in thorns. Over time it learned

that to be beautiful means to be
unjustifiably trusted, and the stranger
the story, the more it's believed
by those with axes and torches. It burned
slowly until the wind picked up
and scattered the seeds.

II. *"Man Disappears into Flower"*

I never saw it. I saw the sound of it.
A piece of fruit slipping into
a shopping bag. Champagne poured
from one flute to another. It formed

like a cloud taking on a shape.
It was an envelope
opening, the carcass of the car's frame
heeling after the tires have dug in.

We never found the body. We kept finding
evidence of the body: a sleeping bag
rolled up like a question mark—
a statement to the police.

It wasn't long before we didn't believe
anything that had to do with him.
Hair color. Hometown.
All we had was the sound

of description, the flat plate of the newspaper,
our words read back to us.
Where he fell, there was a giant flower
closing its petals. . . . A picture

of the flower, hacked open,
bulb empty, a puddle beneath it
one deputy describes as sugary.
It was a mystery we were placed inside

and we became mysterious.
It was difficult to lift
a water glass without feeling
the weight of it.

III. *The Tree That Feeds on Sins*

> *who's to say what's grace*
> *& what's cruelty*
>
> —RIO CORTEZ

Once a year, when flowers bloom
and burn like candles in the evening,
when the tide brings back pieces
of the homes we lost to ruin,

we push them, one by one, into
the tree that feeds on sins.
We aren't proud of what we do.
The world's pain is not mysterious.

Each of us owns a portion
on the skin and underneath,
a discrete series of wounds
with taxonomies and dates.

If we could invent a machine
that eats pain first, and the body after,
we would have to. But we don't have to
because we have the tree.

It tears the knives out by their handles,
ungrooms the brides, rips

the memories from their reels
and melts the plastic spools.

Little known fact: they volunteer.
They line up with their broken limbs
and solemn faces, and solemnly, we grace them.
We aren't proud of what we do.

Soda Can

Shall I uncrumple this much-crumpled thing?

—WALLACE STEVENS

On the cusp of the year, I'm eating a reheated
bagel at a Starbucks on the southern
end of a shopping plaza named after
its own developer. Descartes was right—
the soul enters the body carbonated, then
the body is shaken, sealed, and dropped
from the ether onto earth's outer crust.
No wonder whenever I speak it sounds
exactly like someone else, when I fall in love
it's the opposite of the way I feel. I marvel
at people who can make themselves throw up.

When I fill out my tax return, under
occupation I write *musician*.
Composer is too confusing for them.
When people ask what I do, I say, *I
obliterate Germanic tradition,*
then pat them on the head. I'm very tall.
I wear corduroy and berets. I smell
like peat, like a forest burning in the rain.
In any size room, my voice carries.
I terrify members of all sexes.
They, not I, know not what I do.

I like soda. The sticky, self-clogged
essence, the hideous machine that spits it,
like the passing of a stone, into a tray—
how the crisp eruption of its voice
protests the opening, as if this wasn't
part of the transaction, as if I were
powerful. Someone in a boardroom thought
this up, then ordered a man like my father
to engineer the aluminum to pop
and hiss when it breaks, and always in the same
fragile manner. Every can contains this.

One learns the scrawl of notes and then begins
to hear things. One hears things and orders
their arrangement across a span of time.
One scrawls them out neatly on fine paper
then finds musicians with the sense to play them.
One hears things one once heard only inside,
and they sound different, distorted. One begins
to believe the world destroys everything
it gets its hands on—but hears this abstractly,
like a streak across the corner of the eye.
One scrawls things down across a span of time.

I take a break for America's drink—
the mass-produced soda. It's true, one can't
have a world with Webern but without Coke.
I once said to a crowd of students

that composition could not be taught,
and one stood and asked, quite logically, how
I could do something for a living
that I didn't believe in. *My dear boy*, I said,
that's the definition of maturity.
Why do people always laugh
when I'm trying to be serious? I tried

to write a song that lasted longer than
the mind's ability to remember, a song
of oblivion, but I failed, stopping
at five hours; at best, it only *feels* like forever.
Life tastes good! I might have said.
I might have gone into advertising.
I might have made a child with my wife
on a blanket in a field and handed
down my brand, the logo of my face.
Teach a man to fish, the Lord said.
Our Lord, who never laid eyes upon an ocean,

or anything else that runs past the limits
of the eye, the ear, the mind, anything
that when touched, shatters the toucher,
that, tasted, scatters the tongue's language.
I met her on the day my marriage ended
like the tide offering up some new kind
of water to the sand, or maybe just the same
water repackaged. When they discontinued

New Coke, they called the old Coke
Coke Classic. When Webern moved
to Salzburg, he thought he would be safer.

The boy who shot him drank himself to death
though he'd probably done a favor for
old Webern, who had just learned his only son
had been shot up like Swiss cheese on a train.
(Forgive me if I compare everything to food.
It seems the only remedy for suffering.)
Everything Webern ever wrote fits on six
compact discs, everyone he ever loved
in one small grave. The can is made to match
the size of the hand that will hold it.
Imagine if the eye could hold an ocean.

Against Detroit

Let's move to Detroit she said,
her leg overtop of mine
in the bar.

·

She said, *Use your phone
as a flashlight*, the darkness turning
purple beneath her hand.

·

Dark is the most common adjective
found in poems. The second
is silent.

·

Nothing is completely
dark or absolutely
silent.

·

The more boring a piece of art is
the easier it is to explain it;
hence also to praise it.

·

I've never been to Detroit
but it sounds boring because
everyone loves it so much.

·

I want to read
a book of selected poems
that contains only one poem.

·

By reading that poem aloud
with a particular intonation, the reader unlocks
another poem. And so on.

·

The best part of an orgasm
is that afterwards, I don't feel
like having another one.

·

Producing art doesn't seem to
exhaust anyone. What exhausts them
is talking about producing it.

·

Whenever I told you
I was busy
I was masturbating.

·

It was obnoxious when Boulez said
the solution to opera
was to bomb the opera houses.

·

Feldman also did certain things
to get a rise out of an audience.
Music wasn't one of them.

•

The sharpest turn I can think of
in a contemporary poem is in
Boland's "Atlantis."

•

Someone should define
where a turn becomes
a leap.

•

If you've read the book,
no matter how you felt about it,
it's one of your influences.

•

We fell asleep beneath
the stuffed goose and woke
beneath the stuffed goose.

•

Feldman had four wives,
three mistresses,
and no children.

•

I once made a list of everyone
I'd slept with and realized later
I'd forgotten about someone.

•

Lying to your therapist
is dumb and a waste of money,
but I do it anyway.

•

Scientists estimate you
can only stay in love
for eighteen months.

•

They should also specify:
with the same person,
consecutively.

•

In interviews, Feldman hardly
ever mentions love
or romance.

•

In *Distant Star*, the armless
man turns the pages
of the book with his tongue.

•

She asked me if
I still loved her like crazy,
or just regular.

●

Music's tragedy,
Feldman said, is that it begins
with perfection.

Fugue 52

I.

I was sitting and reading
when the ache came over me.
It was Feldman—
his thin tie and square glasses
cigarette dwarfed by fingers
the elegant wave of his hair.
There he was, chatting with Cage
at the corner bar that stands for all corner bars.
It was early in the afternoon.
They sat in a booth by the window
drinking coffee.
Somewhere, a beautiful woman was dying
but they were unperturbed
flicking their words across the table
like the heads of matchsticks.

II.

It was Feldman drinking coffee.
I was sitting and reading
the elegant wave of his hair.
They sat in a booth by the window
flicking their words across the table
when the ache came over me.
Somewhere, a beautiful woman was dying:
thin tie, square glasses
cigarette dwarfed by fingers.
It was early in the afternoon
at the corner bar that stands for all corner bars
but they were unperturbed
like the heads of matchsticks.
There he was, chatting with Cage.

III.

Somewhere a beautiful woman was dying
like the heads of matchsticks.
There he was chatting with Cage
cigarette dwarfed by fingers.
It was early in the afternoon.
They sat in a booth by the window
but they were unperturbed.
I was sitting and reading
at the corner bar that stands for all corner bars,
flicking their words across the table—
his thin tie and square glasses—
drinking coffee
when the ache came over me.
The elegant wave of his hair.
It was Feldman.

Jack Gilbert

Love is everything
though of course love dies
leaving you in agony
and then you die
and worms crawl in and out of your skull.

But the alternative is worse—

Mope around, hate yourself,
and then die. Worms
will still crawl in and out of your skull
whether or not you stood on top
of the White Mountains to watch
the sun explode into the Sea of Crete
or tasted the skin of a woman
soaked in sweat and wine.

Drink this wine, the Lord said.
I made it myself
with a knife and my arm.

Against Surrealism

A cripple passes by holding a child's hand
After that I'm going to read André Breton?

—CÉSAR VALLEJO

The trees are blackened with trash bags, and the sidewalk is black. At the door is an Argentine composer. In 1978, after a heart transplant, she woke with a mild case of amnesia, enough that she didn't recognize her own music, declared it the work of an insane person, and started over again. Don't get confused. You have not entered Shea Stadium. Snow is not falling inside. Those boxes are not going to fold themselves. All the children are wearing striped polos for a reason known only to the girl you are in love with, who has a gigantic gap between her front teeth and holds a lacrosse stick across her collarbone like an ax. Every year, four hundred people die by accidentally getting rolled into carpets and forgotten. You have lost the hand you were holding when you entered. Did you let go of it, or did it let go of you? This question is written on the ceiling. Your body is a mannequin made from the spare parts of horses. The girl is twirling the lacrosse stick. Is she beckoning you with it? Pine needle after pine needle falls through the horizon, each arriving in the shape of a car. The Argentine opens the doors and tucks each child in, buckles the belt, tests the belt. The girl you love stands and smooths her skirt across her legs. She is going to leave you. She is going to leave you the lacrosse stick. Instead of going down, the sun disappears. There are no cars anywhere now; all the children are gone and the buildings are dark. The Argentine is smoking on the corner. *Are you leaving, too?* you ask. *More than anything*, she says, *I don't want to start over again.*

Examining a Carpet

I'll lie here awhile until you return—
under the fan, uncurling like a fern

on the damp floor of the jungles you left for.
From just one loom come infinite patterns

or so says the last bottle of sauternes,
the phonograph drunk on a single record.

I grew up with the sound of a floor loom,
the treadles banging as the shuttle turned

back and forth between the heddles.
My grandmother's took up half the living room.

In Turkey, wool comes from altitude,
but it's the city that holds the patterns

in its memory. Lose one, lose all
the artistry, no matter how much silk goes in.

It's a fine life wool leads while it lasts,
riding the sheep's thick coat of fat

until shorn into symmetrical stars,
florals, and arabesques—sacred threads

that do the work that fails the tongue—
Procne's son inside the cauldron's urn.

No god could have dyed a color this blue;
it requires an imperfect concern,

sitting down to the same task every day,
memory unspooling in a wordless pool,

the moon's robe falling whole and threadless,
colors rising—abrash—from the sunlight.

Who can say to where they disappear?
I'll lie here awhile until you return.

Mexico

When he thought he was about to encounter Christ, the poet
threw away the last of his heroin.

In Paris, he carried a knife beneath his shirt,
and, without warning, would stab it into the nearest tree.

·

The other poets lied.
They said the poet killed herself after falling in love with a boatman.

That wasn't true.

She grew old and died
in her daughter's bed.

·

A shaman described the poet's body
as *shot through with lightning*.

·

When the storm was at its worst, the poet undressed
and walked out to address the lightning—

Thou art the thing itself, the poet said.

·

The poet believed the self was its own oracle
and became the thing the oracle warned against.

·

To create an anthology
the poet solicited two groups
of people: his friends, and the people
he wanted as his friends.

•

The movement died
not because it went out of fashion
but because the war killed
all of its poets.

•

For the poet, becoming
a good poet meant necessarily becoming
a good person.

But as soon as he became a good person
he ceased being a good poet.

•

To excerpt someone else's words, the poet said,
is a form of begging.

To bring dignity to poetry
we must first bring dignity
to other forms of begging.

•

The poet said,
More poets fail from lack of character
than lack of intelligence.

Which was certainly true of the poet.

•

The poet invented the alphabet
and brought it to the king, saying,

I have created an elixir that will make the people wiser.

But the king replied,
No, you have created the opposite.

•

When the banquet hall collapsed, the lone
survivor was the poet.

The bodies of the other guests were crushed
and mangled, and their families wept
because they could not recognize their dead.

But the poet remembered where all four hundred
had been sitting and, walking through the wreckage,
named the corpses one by one.

•

The poet believed the body
was a sunken ship

unable to prevent the ocean from passing through

a place where even the sharks felt at home.

•

There are some people for whom
no real profession exists, the poet wrote

in a letter to his father. *I count myself*
as one of them.

•

The poet died while ice skating with a friend.

Some lumberjacks
heard them screaming but by the time
they reached the lake, no one was there

just a hole in the ice in the shape of an ear.

•

In the Talmud, the poet invented an angel
and named it Forgetfulness.

•

By writing poems, the poet believed
she could extract the madness from her head

like the doctor in the Hieronymus Bosch painting
who augurs the stone.

And the poet did
and died from doing it.

●

The poet got into the car with the intention
of driving to Mexico

but at the entrance
to the Golden Gate Bridge, parked
and walked out to the middle.

Why drive all the way to Mexico
when Mexico is just over the railing?

●

Every morning, in front
of the mirror, the poet had a routine—

I am a briefcase, he said,
In a crowded train station.

And he put himself down
and walked away.

Now a Word about Twentieth-Century Music

> *... A great number of people, at least in some*
> *places, spent their lives with their wretched bod-*
> *ies strapped to looms made of wooden frames*
> *and rails, hung with weights, and reminiscent of*
> *instruments of torture or cages. It was a peculiar*
> *symbiosis which, perhaps because of its relatively*
> *primitive character, makes more apparent than*
> *any later form of factory work that we are able*
> *to maintain ourselves on this earth only by being*
> *harnessed to the machines we have invented. That*
> *weavers in particular, together with scholars and*
> *writers with whom they had much in common,*
> *tended to suffer from melancholy and all the evils*
> *associated with it, is understandable given the*
> *nature of their work, which forced them to sit bent*
> *over, day after day, straining to keep their eye on*
> *the complex patterns they created.*
>
> —W. G. SEBALD

It rots. On its own tree
no less. False promises of love and worse:
rape; murder. Peace: a word
for something besides peace—a moment,
a respite, the cool flavor of a salve
poured across the tongue, fresh
raspberries and cinnamon wavering beneath
the surface, new wine into old skins.
Let it slowly fill your chest, Lost Soul,
fallen like the rest of us from the garden's
uppermost branches and left for dead, then

saved and given music, food and drink—
this is the tradition we proudly pass down.
This is Morton Feldman. This is Royal Crown.

This is Royal Crown. This is you
beside the roar of the family hearth,
feet stockinged and propped on an ottoman,
pipe shoved slantwise in your mouth,
your wife, beautiful and supine inside
the tasseled arms of a Turkish rug,
the children with their grandparents
for the weekend, an open bottle of RC
in the ice bucket. Now, throw on some
music: Morton Feldman's *Piano*
and String Quartet—79 minutes
of shimmering near-silence and woe.
Relax. Feel your heart's armor melt down.
Listen to Feldman! Drink Royal Crown!

Drink Royal Crown! Listen to Feldman!
Walk with him through postwar Berlin;
fans asking for autographs on albums
as if he were V. I. Lenin and not the Ringo
of the New York School, a Ukrainian
Jew who cannot take a step in Kreuzberg
without feeling what kind of voices pool
beneath the paving stones. *They scream at me!*
he says, and rides the tram staring at

the tracks, the wires tumescent with
electricity, pine trees bleeding sap,
and every guttural voice—though friendly—
calling up the faces of the drowned.
(This message brought to you respectfully.)

Buy Royal Crown! Listen to Feldman's
Intersection for Magnetic Tape.
Feel bored? Confused? For $19.99
our scholars will explain all hundred
and something scores to you
in the privacy of your own home with RC's
Feldman: It's Not an Inquisition! tapes.
Call the number on your television,
and in four to six weeks, we'll deliver
a lifetime's worth of Feldman know-how
in fun, easy-to-listen-to lectures
you can take to the gym, or let soak in
while driving to that job you're better than.
(Limited time offer. Copyright Royal Crown.)

Copyright Morton Feldman for all
the times on commuter trains when
Journey's "Don't Stop Believin'" faded out
and nothingness seemed to take its place—
a cavernous auxiliary silence hidden
in a kink in the headphone wires
but no, the screen says, "Crippled Symmetry"

whatever the fuck that means. Don't you
feel high-minded as you turn the volume up,
bending like a hummingbird to a flower?
But still the notes feel like stars
seen from underwater, in goggles, at noon.
You'd rather not work so hard for sound,
would rather eat, sleep, and drink Royal Crown.

Eat, sleep, and drink Royal Crown.
Eat, sleep, and drink Royal Crown.
We could say it a thousand times. We could
say it consecutively for four or five hours—
a minimalist score for double bassoon
and bass, and after a while it would mean
something different, it would mean that even
after you stopped listening, you were still
listening, would mean you're thirsty
for meaning, for an antecedent
to the thing you'd rather not admit:
you're bored of not believing and will
believe most anything if it arrives with
the right name and the proper asymmetry.

Episode four: "The Bittersweet Symphony"—
Elaine meets and dates a composer
who travels via old-timey bicycle,
wears a black beret that annoys Jerry,
takes Kramer to an avant-garde circus,

teaches George the finer points of carpet
weaving. During a surprise vacation to Boca
Raton, the composer proposes.
Elaine says yes. He confesses he's sterile.
Elaine comes home. End of episode.
End of another evening alone, the computer
still open and glowing on the frameless
mattress in the smoke-ridden apartment—
Great heaps of light chaff before the whirlwind.

Things doctors once prescribed: opium,
cocaine, morphine, leeching, seizures,
lobotomies, mercury, trepanation.
Sometimes people were pronounced dead
and buried alive—fingernail gashes
in the lids of unearthed coffins.
Doctors cut into the wrong thing; allergies
misrepresented on the forms, or the forms
mixed up and the patients poisoned;
doctors operating drunk or on drugs;
house keys and pens dropped into the body
then the body sewed up; the elderly
raped; infants mixed up, lost, or smothered;
bodies thrown into the ocean from cruise ships.

From cruise ships! In international zones,
and the families can't investigate or prosecute.
No one is responsible in an inter-

national zone. No one falls in love or
gets tenure and becomes professor so-and-so
teaching a zero-one, drinking chianti
at the dean's house with Salman Rushdie,
a rare book collection in the living room
next to the hi-fi and a painting of Jerusalem
at sunset. No one shows up late to a reception
with his name on the invitation. No one
teaches music for a living and declares
that music cannot be taught. No one drinks
Royal Crown or listens to Morton Feldman's music.

Feldman. Born: Queens, New York, 1926,
an artist who refused to drink Pepsi
and composed a lot of quiet music, you might
recall he was friends with John Cage,
bonus points for knowing how many
children he had: none. So we are all
his children, sipping RC Cola from a straw
at a corner deli, our hair in pigtails,
reading Primo Levi. We can hear him now
telling us how little he cares for us,
itself a form a caring, a form of belief
in the future of being human. *You
do not have to be good*, the poet said.
Oh yes you do. Oh yes you do.

How the New York School Was Formed

Franz Kline was drunk and listening to *Wu-Tang: Enter the 36 Chambers*.
He said, *Hey Philip Guston, have you heard Wu-Tang?*
Of course I've heard Wu-Tang, says Guston.
Jackson Pollock gave it to me. I think he burned it
from O'Hara. Then Rauschenberg walked in.
Is that Schoenberg? he said.
No, it's Wu-Tang, they said. Then John Cage walked in.
Then Cleanth Brooks. Then Garth Brooks
and Tammy Wynette. They were all smoking dope,
listening to Wu-Tang and painting.
This is how the New York School was formed.

Two Epigraphs without a Poem

Right under the title I've written what is called an
epigraph. An epigraph is a quotation from some
older book, or poem, or story, or anything that's
written by some wiser person. Poets sometimes
copy epigraphs under the titles of their poems, so
that the souls of the wise men, or the saints, will
help them to make a good poem. An epigraph is
like a prayer.

—JAMES WRIGHT, in a letter to his son Franz

Just about every boy on my team has a pair of
baseball spikes. I sure wish you would send me
$5.00 so I could get a pair. They help you grip the
ground when your running.

—FRANZ WRIGHT, in a letter to his father

Poems about Concentration
for People Who Can't Concentrate

Imagine a deer in headlights.
Loop that image.
Now imagine watching the loop.

•

You're at your desk.
You can't concentrate.
Imagine if not concentrating
was concentrating.

•

That time you took drugs
and thought a piece of tin foil stapled to the wall
was a fish tank. But why
was there a piece of tin foil stapled to the wall?

•

Two people, naked, in a gondola
suspended over Mount Blanc.
Lightning strikes the tower, shorting the wires.
Wind and snow shake the gondola.
The two people are you
and your infant daughter.

•

You're trying to think about your child
but you keep thinking about yourself.
Imagine you're the child.

•

Imagine you're a gondola in a blizzard.
Imagine the blizzard is inside the gondola.
Let go of the wire.

Orange and Life in General

Noise does no good. The good makes no noise.

—NICCOLO CASTIGLIONI

The night the news about the blizzard came
he paid a friend to sleep inside his car
so that in the morning, when the car was buried,
someone would be inside to honk the horn,
and he would be outside to record what a car horn
sounded like buried beneath snow.

Parable #1: a man gets stuck inside a blizzard—
something that cuts the world down to its essence.
Afterwards, he says, I've haven't been living.
From now on, the whole world is my blizzard.
But the world is the world, and he spends the rest
of his life reminiscing about the blizzard.

Parable #2: At a party in New York, she's
the most beautiful thing in the world to him.
*I wouldn't sleep with you if you were the last person
on earth*, she says. *Then don't sleep with me*,
he says, *but come over and have some tea.*
And she does. And that's when the blizzard hits.

When the power returned after the New
York City blackout, sixty thousand
people had left their spouses for coworkers,
neighbors, nannies, and doormen.

Does the world teach us our essence? Or is
our essence what we teach the world?

Note to self: Watch more *Boy Meets World.*
Note to world: imagine if, instead of
ringing, a phone made the sound of a person
screaming. Every car horn, someone
screaming. Every television. Music
would be the sound of two people screaming.

He used to fall asleep at the movies
and then have to guess what was happening
when he woke up: she's an orchard's caretaker,
he's a textbook salesman who has run out
of textbooks. They're walking to an aquifer.
All the horses are gone from earth.

When the phone rings, how does he know
that it's you? Is it you? Or is it
the thing inside of him that wants it
to be you? If he picks up the receiver
and hears your voice, will he be able
to tell the difference? Parable #3.

At the party they go around and name
their favorite color and their greatest fear.
Mauve Death goes home with White Wilderness.
Green Drowning wants Black Marriage

but settles for Blue Acid. Pink Failure
spills merlot on Orange Life in General.

The phone rings. It's the voice of someone
who isn't afraid of anything, but to you
it sounds like screaming. If it doesn't
start snowing soon, she is going to leave you.
People used to make it snow by dancing.
You can make it snow by falling asleep.

O, 1987

How you nested in the bones of '86
and ate your way out with a fork and knife,
napkin tucked into your oxford, not spilling
a single day. How you waited
at the end of the long, narrow dock
(with boards missing where the ring might fall through)
as the wedding party froze under
the sun in pressed linen, dead flowers
in their lapels, heads upright, ingesting
each word from the priest's mouth
like a medicine blue against
       the white sky's tray of paper cups.

How could we know you were waiting
in the idling car's back seat, wrapped
in old newspaper, one eye leaking out,
locked in place and reeking of bone
and salt and rot, as the rain died on the glass
and ran into shallow puddles where
the flies rose and, smelling you, threw
themselves against the windshield's face—
how safe you'd made yourself inside
our world. Distracted by one another,
       we never suspected you.

And when the rain left, how you swam up
the retreating clouds into the sky's narrowing

hole, not an ascension but a sucking,
a high-pitched screech immiscible with
the sound of our twin selves asleep on the earth—
atonal is too human to describe it;
more like *asanguine*, a score for brass orchestra
by the nothing that it wasn't. Nothing
was us in October. Nothing was the crown
of night-struck buildings. For four months
I sat yearless on the beach, waiting

   but nothing didn't come. Just 1988.

Dear Goose

No one had to hear you sing to know
you'd be killed in an accident.
It was your name, it was those Ray-Bans
you wore like a Halloween mask.

Lorca said, *Whoever fears death*
carries death on his shoulders.
But death carried you.
Death has a yellow moustache

and plays volleyball with Lorca
shirtless or in unbuttoned shirts,
the dog tags of his beloved
dangling from a chain of sins.

Death's specialty is omelets
and karaoke from a bar's old piano.
He can open up a man
like an egg, a song, or a parachute.

Bidart & Lowell

After you were dead, I worked
nonstop at night sewing
your poems back together, or where
necessary, pulling them
apart, subsisting on tear-

and-eat items at the gas station
on the corner, push-button
milkshakes and microwaveable
popcorn. My body
was a suit I picked out

every morning and every
night hung back up
inside the closet, surrounded by
your weightlessness, at once
heavy and useless,

one foot still a little longer
than the other, a dead father
and mother, the history
of cinema before 1960 playing
on loop inside my brain.

One day, I'm Janet Gaynor
in the Parisian sewers; another,
I'm the mountain in *The Searchers*

John Wayne is walking toward
and then I'm the ranch house door

that closes on itself to consecrate
the darkness, the border
between the country of loss
and the country of time.
O my mentor, my minotaur—

the hospital where you held
my hand is gone, and with it
the labyrinth and the latticework,
the chandeliers of tubes,
the horrible food, the buffet

of ways to be dead and still falling
in love with how the light blinds
the television, how the body stays
exactly where you leave it,
laid across the crux of sheets

like Helen Hayes in *A Farewell
to Arms*, a pillow for an aureole,
and no one to lift you up,
so I lift you up now—
I take your body

to the cherry blossoms
in the window, the bell choir,
the lake thawing in the valley.
You weigh almost nothing.
My arms are giving way.

Noir

In *Out of the Past*
Robert Mitchum flees

to the smallest town in Mexico
but there she is
at the bar, sipping a martini.

•

He knows
he's a dead man, a cut-out
made of iron,

and goes to where
all dead men go:

San Francisco, California.

•

He wears cargo pants
and a pocket watch
and drinks

overpriced mojitos
in Mission pool halls.

He wears out the country
music buttons on the jukebox
at Sadie's Flying Elephant.

•

No one tells him:
Mitchum, the movie's over.
Jane Greer's in a coffin.

No one tells him
the pocket watch is not
endearing.

Who Was Sonia Sekula?

Art in America, *October, 1971;*
Photograph by André de Dienes, Mid-1940s

By how she holds her head, I can feel the photographer's fingers
positioning her chin, can hear him dragging the wicker chair

from the back of the porch out into the sun
where it breaks apart the shadows created by the house.

He rummaged on the beach until he found a piece of driftwood
to lean against the porch's edge. He unhooked

a curtain from its rod, ring by ring, wrapped it around her,
and handed her the rod to hold like a scepter.

He wanted her to appear to be naked underneath.
He wanted men, opening the magazine, to fall in love.

Against her body, the editors juxtaposed her paintings.
They pulled paragraphs, like teeth, from her diary.

During a vacation in Crete, she writes, *Usually,*
you fall into bed alone, hungry and sad and drunk,

and each night it's the loneliest night in the week.
Her friends, when quoted, seem relieved to hear she's dead.

She was part Hungarian. Her mother drove to Zurich,
collected the body, and buried it in St. Moritz.

I Drank Some Milk and It Rained

The sun set over the balcony.
I opened a beer.
It rained.
You came downstairs.
We played solitaire
by lamplight.
The phone rang.
Sonia came down.
There was a knock
and seven or eight more entered.
There was a knock.
There were people
in the living room,
the hallway, the bedroom,
the bathroom, there were
people in the kitchen.
Someone brought a radio.
Someone brought a ukulele.
Someone joined hands
with someone else.
Someone stood to sing.
Someone sang.
Wine bottles were opened
and piled in the sink.
Someone yelled out
the score of the Yankees game.

Someone yelled out
Preston Sturges has died.
Someone yelled out
Suzanne Vega is born!
And then it was just you
and me playing gin rummy.
And then it was just me,
a magazine tented over
my eyes. The sun
rose over the balcony.
I drank some milk
and it rained.

Origin Myth

In the beginning, there was the surface—
an unbroken wave of absence.

Night was the backs of their eyelids.
Darkness was a brightness.

To raise the scaffolding and carve
a depth into the flatness

they dragged the corners to the center,
a wreath of pipes, boards, and bolts

stretching up into the ether
where the edge was held together.

It's hard to build a sky from underneath.
You have to learn a language.

You have to step on one another.
The worst was learning how to fall asleep

or else be left alone inside the web
of thoughts that spun whenever

the sky just hung there above them
half-finished, full of holes and rips

where light came through and made
the shapes of cups and bowls and bears,

the design itself haphazard and spontaneous,
the sturdiest parts part-accidents,

and the rest just tape and glue. In retrospect
it looks hand-drawn, fictional almost,

like how the water regains its shape
after swallowing a boat.

A Story about a Marriage

A plumber came to snake the drain.
Big snake or little snake? he said.
And so we bought a snake. The water
disappeared like water down the drain.

A friend of a friend of a friend
gave us the name of a guy in Kendall
who maybe had something we'd like.
The snake came in a plastic cage.

It was black with brown spots,
or brown with black spots, and thinner
than my thumb. We named it
Horace but that was not its name.

Horace loved the sun. He loved to lie
on my wife's convex belly as my wife
lay on the chaise lounge in a bikini
reading the Styles section

of the Sunday edition of the paper.
He loved to eat and grow and hide
in dark places like piles of towels,
and showers, and dirty laundry,

and the blankets on the bed where
the dog slept when we were at work.
Perhaps it was because he loved the dog
that we loved him. Boris loved the sun

too and curled up with Horace
in the warm spots on the floor.
Horace nuzzled Boris and Boris
cleaned his eyes with his tongue.

When Horace outgrew the biggest
cage, we gave him his own room
and a thousand watts of light.
The new baby slept with us.

His name was Horace too.
What we didn't expect was how
Horace One, now twenty feet long
and thick as a trunk, could move

from room to room. As if
he'd never grown, the police said,
he could flatten himself and go
underneath the doors. I remember

I'd dreamt of something: the plumber
drilling the big snake into my ear
because there were some leaves
stuck in my head that kept

the thoughts from moving freely.
I woke up refreshed.
My wife was still asleep.
Horace was lying in the sun.

O, 1951

.In all things, the rendition's
what matters—paper lanterns strung too low,
a too-spiked punch bowl, the threesome of freshmen
singing The Orioles: *It's too soon to know*,
my arm as it circumnavigates your back
and pulls you closer, the view of the gold
cross around your neck, the moon asking
permission from the gym to glow, the Greek
vacation your parents took, their bedroom
forbidden and cavernous, the sound
of buttons as they lose their grip, how
your tongue says, *You can't stay*
        then seems to forget.

    How the sun arrives
with nowhere else to go, how we strip
and wash the linen, sit naked on the balcony—
me smoking, you declaiming on the history
of the park, how the designer's death between
the plan's completion and the city's review
allowed his vision to pass unaltered, hence
the view, hence why I remember how
the mulberries were planted to frame the lake
and shade the bathers resting on its edge,
and why I remember how the berries tasted—
I picked a few on the way to the train—
like every hour of their making measured
        and compressed.

Anecdote

A distinguished neurologist was consulted one day by a new patient. *What seems to be the problem?* he asked. The patient complained about the stress of living in East Berlin in the late 1990s—the secret bars in abandoned buildings, the cheap, high-quality drugs, the all-night toggling between music, conversation, and sex. *I have the overwhelming feeling of being a part of some historical moment*, the patient said. The doctor examined him thoroughly and replied, *There's nothing wrong with you. You just need to relax—try doing something low-brow for a change. Go see a concert by that guy Garth Brooks, and life will feel different. Ah, but Doctor*, answered the patient, *I am Garth Brooks.*

Easter Eggs

I.

A Japanese programmer, while in the final development stages for Konami's *Contra*, learned of the death of Morton Feldman. Overcome with grief, he inserted a cheat code as a memorial. Press down, down, up, up, right, left, right, left, A, B as the game is loading, and the soundtrack becomes an 8-bit version of *Rothko Chapel*. Make it all the way to level eight, and the final boss is Pierre Boulez with two ukuleles.

II.

On January 12th, type "Morton Feldman unborn child" into Google, and the screen goes black for four hours.

III.

On a third generation iPod, make a playlist of these songs in this exact order:

The Outfield, "Your Love"
Ledbelly, "Where Did You Sleep Last Night"
David Byrne, "Once in a Lifetime"
Bonnie Raitt, "Something to Talk About"
Phish, "Julius"
Gregg Allman, "I'm No Angel"
Eric B. & Rakim, "Paid in Full"

Press shuffle. An unreleased recording of Morton Feldman singing A-ha's "Take on Me" at a karaoke bar in Buffalo, NY, will play first, followed by the entirety of *Led Zeppelin II*.

IV.

Go to Carnegie Hall. In the restroom adjacent to the green room, look into the mirror, and say *Oriental carpets* three times, then turn out the lights. Turn them back on and an unpublished Feldman score is written in lipstick on the mirror.

V.

In Vienna, make love to your wife in a street-facing room of the Hotel Sacher Wien. During climax, scream out, *The glockenspiel is a serious instrument!* Nine months later, your wife will give birth to a son. Name him after yourself.

Projection 2

Score by Morton Feldman, 1951

The names of the instruments are written on the left-hand side
in capitalized letters: TRUMPET, PIANO,
FLUTE, VIOLIN, CELLO, each corresponding
to a row of boxes connected with black lines
or dotted ones, and inside the boxes, only a blankness
or a geometric shape. Someone, an uncle

or an intern, has confused the papers
in his drawer. This is not a score.
It's a schematic blueprint for a museum dedicated
to preserving the culture of roadside motels.
Here's where the exhibition of scratchy towels goes.
Here is the wall of landscape paintings.
Here's the old woman who runs the place, asleep
in her office, her head on top of her hands.

Scores are often louder than their music.
It's all those symbols crammed into succession.
It's the promise that inside there might exist
some form of happiness or elation.

But not in here.

In the bottom corner, the name of the composer
is cut out of the paper like a decorative hedge.

In the intersection outside the motel's entrance,
a traffic light decorates the evening
yellow, then yellow, then yellow.

Qasida of the Pinecone

after Lorca

The pinecone
wasn't asking for the dawn:
almost undead on its limb,
it asked to be alone.

The pinecone
wasn't asking for science or shadow:
the mind's and body's limits,
it asked to be alone.

The pinecone
wasn't asking for the pinecone:
the stillness of the sky was in it;
it asked to be alone.

Florida Man

On a terrace in Cincinnati, Donald Justice.
Cincinnati with its Hungarian street parades
and Applebee's propped against one another
like books; the fracturing of the Hungarians
and their bakeries. Goodbye to the Szabos and Kovaches.
Goodbye to the fishermen and their fishes,
      Bette Midler singing a slowed-
      down version of "Jolene"
      in the Cincinnati Convention Center.
Cincinnati in the car, leaning its head
out the window on the way to San Francisco—
San Francisco, who has never even heard
of Cincinnati, has barely heard of Berkeley or Oakland,
that thing between the mountains and the shipping cranes.

Last night I ordered a hang glider from Australia.
It took me three months but I made a flipbook
of the '86 World Series and pasted my face over
Mookie Wilson's. Whenever an airplane passes, I press
my genitals to the cold surface of the window glass.
I reconnect the neighborhoods of Los Angeles
with cobblestone avenues that wind up the hills
to the Getty, where I am Eloise, living in the olive trees,
eating bagels the size of elephants.

Dear Board of Directors, I have emptied out
all the old feelings. From the top
of the church, I can see where the land pretends to recede

and, dipping, accepts the river. I can see why the church
becomes its spire, why the drug addicts and pigeons
circle around the diner on the corner. I can see the edge
of the peninsula where the halls of Saint Andrew
smell like a flood of semen had risen and retreated;
can see the black clouds of the fire closing in
from where a man filled a soda can with kerosene
and tossed it at an alligator. I pull
my backpack, drawn upon in gold and black marker,
closer to my back. This is my backpack.
There are many others like it, but this one is mine.

In the gymnasium, a man with one eye instructs us
not to shoot heroin, to toss our Ouija boards
into the garbage, to watch closely as the shuttle pew-pews
into the sky, breaks apart, and disappears
into the firmament, a single firework lobbed underhand
by Okeechobee's open fist, each pair of eyes
stuck like sliding glass doors fallen off their tracks.

O, terracotta giving way to Chattahoochee.
O, Tomasso's Pizza, O, landscape crews
with names that pun on nature, whose Zodiac is this,
dragged into the dark, fetid canal, and who is that
standing up inside its cavity like Rambo crossing the Delaware,
one pontoon sliced open and bleeding air?

Wagner & Nietzsche

They first met in Wagner's office.
He showed Nietzsche the view of the water.
The younger man looked down and felt dizzy.
Distance is what makes a god.
They could see every border of the city.

Nietzsche must have looked like the water, too:
a thick coat of sunlight across the chrome
of surface and the mystery of depth.
To Nietzsche, Wagner was an office:
the perfect chair, the perfect desk.

The oldest crime on record is a young man
falling in love with an older one.
Another name for it is *fatherhood.*
We know the world is flawed for good
because the world requires it.

Let us gather to celebrate
our fathers, our father says. The world
was better before we entered it.
Every son is a curse carrying
the antidote inside of him.

When Nietzsche stopped coming
to Bayreuth, Wagner's wrath
was sad and comical. In public,

he rebuked his adopted son. In private,
he missed everything about him.

O, Father who is not my Father,
I forgive you, Nietzsche wrote.
I forgive what love coerces you to do.
When the Good Father finds your door,
I will feed his horse a sugar cube.

There Is a Forward Motion in Old Video Games

after Donald Justice

There is a forward motion in old video games
that keeps a character from going back.
When you move, the camera pans from left
to right but stops when you turn back.
Some wall is following. The music keeps playing.

The same opponent appears over and over
trudging toward your fists. The surface is a knot
that tightens on one end while it loosens
on the other. The sky is full of ether.
Tubes lead nowhere. The wall persists.

The world is divided into levels, so it stands
to reason, life was worse in the beginning.
As the dead pile up, the evil thins but in force
increases. The wall was built to keep it
from circling back to the beginning.

The cartridge is dusty, kid. Blow into it.
One day the wall will be torn down and forgotten.
Good and evil will look exactly the same,
and all that we accomplished from dying and saving
will be erased as if we'd never been playing.

Leica

Through the viewfinder's view
a second frame
comes into view
framed by the single panel of the window's edges
where the wood meets the pane
of glass. The eye's ledge

suspends mostly sky
because of the window's height
and the position of her body
on the nearby bed
focused on the light
as it passes through window, camera, eye.

Laundry
dries from the balcony grates
of two facing buildings, like similarly
cut keys, the shirts and sheets
unable to decide if this is waiting or fate
with nothing underneath.

At least the satellite dishes understand
their endings,
waxing full of bland
third acts, fastened fast
to the cracked cement wall's pending
collapse.

Dover Beaches

The sea is a bomb tonight.
The moon illuminates it
like a yard light keeps the yard from going black,
like an embassy flies a single flag, or a church
choir stands in unison to sing.
The sea is an invitation,
a car on fire, an unopened letter.

Long ago, so-and-so heard it
speaking to him through the legs
of a table. You know how
table legs can be unstable, one a little shorter
than the other so the table wobbles?
It's a small thing but it's a reason
to eat hemlock, to put rocks in your pockets,
to run through the temple screaming.

The sea is the earth,
humanless and impenetrable. It swallows
light and air, and deposits what's left
at its outermost exterior, or gathers it
on the surface in swirls the size
of Texas; at its heart, the sea is clean
and cold and uninhabitable.

Love, should we even bother
touching one another? You're married.
I have psoriasis, and we're inside

this Fed-Ex office, making flyers for a pet
we promised to protect, who now
is lost and likely dead, or worse.
The world is a bad, awful, no-good place.
We are the world.

And from the Chimney Issues the Smoke

In 1958, when Cardinal Roncalli was appointed
pope, he wrote in his diary,
Today I was appointed pope.

What is a song?
A rat fleeing a burning building.

Songs, by definition, don't know
how to defend themselves.
Even when claiming power
songs are damaged and powerless.

It has been said that the people of Königsberg
set their watches by Kant's daily walks.
It has been said is the problem with music.

The laziest critical move circulating today
is the comparison of music to other art forms, especially poetry.

Music is at least fifty years behind poetry
and slipping further and further behind.

I heard a boxer on TV once defend the brutality of his profession
by saying: *99% of boxers would give you the shirt off his back.*

I feel the same way about musicians
only the percentage is reversed.

The only convincing reason to put your name
on a song is so that you can sell it.

In the 80s, I read surf magazines
even though I didn't surf.

There was a recurring ad in them I always liked.
It said, *If you don't surf, don't start.*
If you surf, never stop.

Many musicians have stopped composing
because they no longer wanted to do it,
describing it as a dehydration, a drying up
of the notes inside them.

How many surfers have stopped surfing
because it no longer felt good to do it?

I can't remember how it felt to write music
before I started thinking about writing music.

On a talk show the host and his guest, a porn star,
get into an argument about whether there is enough
porn in the world already. Why make more?

I think there's enough, he says.
No, there's not, she says.

I think there should be enough music in the world already.
No, there's not, says the composer.

When the annual story about music not mattering appears
the musicians emerge to defend their art form.

Only by music are we saved from nonsense.

Listening to music is like eating nothing but sugar.

When a critic asked Morton Feldman why
he put only one moment of real beauty
into a composition that lasts four hours, he said,
How many more do you need?

One should be enough, right?

Today I was appointed pope, the Cardinal wrote.

On what day, on what page of your diary
did you appoint yourself?

Maybe it wasn't you
but a collection of your selves.

Do you see them now? Putting on their robes and hats
and locking the door to your body?

There they are, casting their votes,
throwing the paper into the fire.

And from the chimney issues the smoke.

January in Buffalo

The snow in Buffalo blows to and fro
burying cars on the avenue home.
I think that sound, in general, likes to be alone—
boiling pots, ringing phones.

This time of year, I can't leave the windows
open so the television's on—
news from Milwaukee and Tehran.
Youth in masks. Firework season.

The dark blue smell of the heat
and the shadow-flags of the plows.
Someone is shouting for the bus.
Someone else is the reason.